Translated from the Russian by Yuri S. Shirokov

Published and distributed throughout the world by T.F.H. Publications, Inc.

T.F.H. PUBLICATIONS, INC.
211 West Sylvania Avenue
Neptune, NJ 07753

Distributed in the UNITED STATES by T.F.H. Publications, Inc., 211 West Sylvania Avenue, Neptune City, NJ 07753; in CANADA by H & L Pet Supplies Inc., 27 Kingston Crescent, Kitchener, Ontario N2B 2T6; Rolf C. Hagen Ltd., 3225 Sartelon Street, Montreal 382 Quebec; in ENGLAND by T.F.H. Publications Limited, 4 Kier Park, Ascot, Berkshire SL5 7DS; in AUSTRALIA AND THE SOUTH PACIFIC by T.F.H. (Australia) Pty. Ltd., Box 149, Brookvale 2100 N.S.W., Australia; in NEW ZEALAND by Ross Haines & Son, Ltd., 18 Monmouth Street, Grey Lynn, Auckland 2 New Zealand; in SINGAPORE AND MALAYSIA by MPH Distributors (S) Pte., Ltd., 601 Sims Drive, #03/07/21, Singapore 1438; in the PHILIPPINES by Bio-Research, 5 Lippay Street, San Lorenzo Village, Makati Rizal; in SOUTH AFRICA by Multipet Pty. Ltd., 30 Turners Avenue, Durban 4001. Published by T.F.H. Publications, Inc. Manufactured in the United States of America by T.F.H. Publications, Inc.

THE OFFICIAL BOLSHOI BALLET BOOK OF
THE NUTCRACKER

Captions for all the photographs were written by
Dr. Herbert R. Axelrod

By Yuri Grigorovich and Alexander Demidov
Photography by Vladimir Pchalkin

A FOREWORD

This book, on the history of making and the stage life of THE NUTCRACKER, opens a series on the Bolshoi ballet and its present repertoire, in which the past and present are blended in an harmonious whole.

But why THE NUTCRACKER of all ballets?

This ballet is of special significance to us. It came into being on the watershed between two centuries and divided the history of choreographic art in two, as it were. It marked the end of an era and set the stage for the spectacular advance of Russian ballet in the 20th century.

Without THE NUTCRACKER Stravinsky's, Prokofiev's and Shostakovich's ballet scores would have been impossible. This masterpiece of art stimulated a quest of new styles and forms in the sphere of choreography.

Reviewing the history of THE NUTCRACKER today, we can see more clearly the ways of progress followed by Russian choreography and Russian national culture that had laid the groundwork for it.

This touchingly sincere poem of childhood, which has no analogue in world musical literature, has a universal appeal that defies the limits of time and strikes a responsive chord in the hearts of all people regardless of their social outlook on the world.

This ballet stirs our dormant memories of our first dreams of happiness and first feelings. It makes us relive the events that shaped our own emotional experiences and ideas of love and hate, good and evil, forces locked in an endless contest since the dawn of history.

Yuri Grigorovich
Moscow, October 1985

Yuri Grigorovich. 1984.

CONTENTS

N.B. The Russian libretto uses the name "Masha"; the English use Marie, Mary, Marsha and/or Maria. Masha and Marie are used interchangeably in this book.

Supplementary information about the color photographs.

pg. 57 Set of first scene

pg. 58-59 Dance of Snowflakes; 1st act .

pg. 60 set of seventh scene

pg. 61 Set of 4th scene

pg. 63 set of 2nd scene

pg. 64-65 Scene of children's festival; lst act

pg. 66 Nadezhda Pavlova as Marie; 1st act

pg. 67 Parent's ball, 1st act

pg. 68 Yury Vetrov as Uncle Drosselmeier; 1st act

pg. 69 A. Loparevich as Uncle Drosselmeier

pg. 70 Yury Vetrov as Uncle Drosselmeier; 1st act

pg. 71 D. Peregudov as The Clown; 1st act

pg. 72 U. Ternovskaja as the Witch and A. Kedrov as the Devil; lst act

pg. 73 N. Arkhipova as Marie, L. Okhotnikova as Nutcracker doll, Y. Vetrov as Uncle Drosselmeier and O. Vasyuchenko as Marie's brother; 1st act

pg. 74 N. Arkhipova as Marie, Yury Vetrov as Uncle Drosselmeier and L. Okhotnikova as the Nutcracker doll; 1st act

pg. 75 Set of 5th scene

pg. 76 Set of 3rd scene

pg. 77 A. Loparevich as Uncle Drosselmeier; 1st act

14

A 75-Year-Long Path

The ballet *The Nutcracker* belongs to the last, most complicated and tragic period of Tchaikovsky's life and work. He composed it in 1892 after the opera *The Queen of Spades* and shortly before the Sixth Symphony ("Pathetique"), which was first performed in public in 1893, only two weeks before the composer's sudden and mysterious death.

Some events in Tchaikovsky's life warrant a close look at *The Nutcracker*, which was destined to become a component of a great requiem made up of an opera, a ballet, and a symphony. That may account for the mystery of *The Nutcracker* as one of the most beautiful and elusive compositions in the history of ballet music.

This ballet failed to find a worthy embodiment on the stage in the last century, and it has established itself at the modern ballet theatre in the face of enormous difficulties. In fact, until the last production of *The Nutcracker* at the Bolshoi in Yuri Grigorovich's choreography of 1966, the ballet had not known a full-blooded theatrical presentation. Failures that plagued *The Nutcracker*'s productions at times led critics to extravagant conclusions. For instance, Boris Asafiev, a leading Russian composer and musicologist, declared at one time that *The Nutcracker* is, in general, an anti-theatrical composition which cannot be produced on the stage.

Time has shown this statement to be unwarranted, and today *The Nutcracker* is one of the most popular ballets, while Yuri Grigorovich's version, which is well known in many countries, is very high on the list of public favorites. For that, however, Russian ballet has had to traverse a path of seventy-five years.

This photo was prepared upon the completion of his *Nutcracker* music in 1892. The inscription reads: "To Porfiry Gustavovich, in good memory of the concert of January 23, 1893. Signed P. I. Tchaikovsky."

The Phenomenon of The Nutcracker

What gave birth to the phenomenon of The Nutcracker? What shaped the mystery of this ballet which was decades ahead of its time? What makes choreographers wrack their brains about its music on such an unsophisticated and sentimental subject as a little girl's adventures on Christmas Eve?

The main question that has always puzzled ballet critics and choreographers is the message of the ballet. Is it addressed to children or to adult spectators who are led by the composer's fantasy into the world of their own souls? Is it intended to stir their distant memories and make them relive, if only for an instant, their long-forgotten experiences and emotions?

In answering this question theoreticians, the ballet critics, disagreed with practical workers, the choreographers. The former, relying on scientific analysis, realized the dual nature of the ballet, which was simultaneously for the children and about the children by analogy with works of children's literature, such as *Alice in Wonderland* by Lewis Carroll. Practical workers, however, preferred a more concrete solution to the problem and in their quests, down to Yuri Grigorovich's production, inclined to the idea that *The Nutcracker* is a ballet for children alone. Making a choice between its philosophically meaningful music and its naive fairy-tale plot, they opted for the latter, not knowing how the music can be harmonized with the plot.

Practical workers reasoned in simple terms: a spectator comes to the ballet theatre to watch the action, which should be picturesque and fascinating, rather than listen to the music however beautiful it may be. In the opinion of choreographers, the action of *The Nutcracker*, so pleasing to the eye, so touching and entertaining, could fascinate only a young audience. Therefore, until as late as 1966, *The Nutcracker* had been presented at different theatres almost exclusively as a Sunday matinee for children.

As a result, a paradoxical situation developed: Tchaikovsky's other ballets, such as *Swan Lake* and *The Sleeping Beauty*, which are also based on fairy-tale themes, were for some reason considered ballets for adult spectators, whereas *The Nutcracker* with its sophisticated music, superior for its merits to the afore-mentioned works, was stubbornly listed among "school" productions at all theatres.

What were the causes of this discrepancy and who was to blame for that?

These questions could have been unimportant today, if we knew that *The Nutcracker's* stage life had already ended, its mystery unravelled and made clear to all. This ballet, however, will certainly be staged by many other choreographers in the future, and they will have to tackle anew both the old and new problems that constantly arise in connection with it.

Yuri Grigorovich said in this context: *"We would be too self-conceited to believe that The Nutcracker has been revealed to our minds in this century. We are closer to a certain extent to understanding this ballet than last century's choreographers, but this is a flimsy argument in the historical dispute on The Nutcracker, a dispute that will hardly ever be settled."*

Therefore, reviewing the record of productions of this ballet and the history of its composition, we are not only seeking an answer to the problems facing us but also giving practical aid to the future interpreters of *The Nutcracker.*

The Sources

Tchaikovsky composed *The Nutcracker* at a strange time of his life, which was far from anything like the happy dreams of childhood.

He had read Hoffmann's fairy-tale *"The Nutcracker and the Mouse King,"* which provided the basis for the ballet scenario, as far back as 1882, in Florence. In those years the composer lived abroad, mostly in Italy, and Florence was his favorite city.

Tchaikovsky had read *The Nutcracker* in the French translation of Dumas père. Though he admired the fairy-tale, no idea to compose a ballet on this theme crossed his mind at the time. Ten years later he accepted the offer to write the music for a ballet on the theme of *The Nutcracker* from Ivan A. Vsevolozhsky, Director of the Russian Imperial Theatres. The latter, in fact, was the initiator of this theme, while Tchaikovsky himself showed a preference for the ancient German fairy-tale *Ondine,* whose images allured him as long as he lived.

In Tchaikovsky's artistic biography there was a curious detail: he composed his finest operas and ballets, as a rule, on the initiative of other persons, while his own cherished dreams did not come true. He either failed to implement them or his plans came to nothing. For instance, it was Vsevolozhsky who had insisted on his composing *The Sleeping Beauty,* although Tchaikovsky had stubbornly requested an order for *Ondine.*

Less than a year before composing *The Queen of Spades* the composer said in a letter to his brother Modest Tchaikovsky that he was indifferent to that theme and could produce only mediocre music for it.

We know well today that early in 1890 his reluctance to compose that music gave way, in fact, to feverish work at mad speed, with fits of hysteria and tears that resulted in the creation of a great opera in a matter of only forty-four days.

On the other hand, Tchaikovsky's *Ondine* never materialized. He had burnt the score of his early opera on the subject, while all latter plans and scenarios of *Ondine*, now an opera, now a ballet, remained unfulfilled. Nor did he write an opera on the subject of *Romeo and Juliet* by Shakespeare, whose idea he cherished all his life.

At the same time, the subjects he had chosen himself and embodied in music were not very successful or popular. Few people today are familiar with such of his operas as *The Little Shoes* (Cherevichki) or *The Maid of Orléans*, *Mazepa* or *The Sorceress*. Musicologists know of their merits, of course, but the public at large is mostly ignorant of them.

The Nutcracker had a similar destiny.

In the very same Florence where he would write *The Queen of Spades* eight years later he read Hoffmann's fairy-tale and politely put it aside. After some time the wily Vsevolozhsky palmed off this fairy-tale upon him as a ballet scenario, and Tchaikovsky, who probably recollected his impressions of the tale readily, agreed to take it up.

A month later he started to complain about the plot and the libretto, then repeatedly requested the Directorate to put off the deadlines for completing the score, telling his relatives in his letters that this theme was good for nothing, that it was impossible to embody images of the Kingdom of Sweets in music, yet he did compose that music during his sea journey to the United States.

As a result, he came back from America with a score that was practically completed, and, as it was his custom, he now praised his work, but called it worthless.

Speaking in general, one can hardly see much logic in Tchaikovsky's train of thought at the time of composing *The Nutcracker*. All the more paradoxical is the fact that, simultaneously with the *The Nutcracker* which he disliked and hastened to have done with as soon as possible, he was composing the opera *Iolanta*, whose subject greatly fascinated him.

What came of it is well known today. *Iolanta* with its stilted optimism and pseudo-romantic pomp has remained far behind *The Nutcracker*.

An Emotional Conflict

The Nutcracker was an outgrowth of the deep-seated psychological conflict and pent-up emotions that tormented the composer as long as he lived.

This ballet brings into focus his whole life and links together its beginning and its end.

The last years of his life had tragic undertones. At first view he was a successful composer of European renown. He was awarded a doctorate at Cambridge, made frequent guest tours and even visited the New World. He was the first Russian musician to win worldwide fame.

Poverty, a struggle for recognition, quests of a sponsor to have his compositions played in public, were now a thing of the past. He was in his hey-day. What else to desire?

That, however, was too good to be true. In fact, he was an unhappy man plagued by a formidable emotional problem since his youth. He was denied the simple joys of family life by an aberration in his emotional make-up.

As a man of integrity he felt frustrated and betrayed by Nature. That painful discord between dreams and reality largely shaped the psychological discrepancies in his private life and artistic pursuits. The permanent mental strain had ended in a severe nervous breakdown at a young age when he attempted suicide after his hasty and disastrous marriage.

In his letters to his close relatives in the 1870's one can find confessions and many curious psychological details that motivated his later steps.

Almost in every letter Tchaikovsky complains bitterly of his sinful nature, which is "an obstacle to a happy life", and says that it is his "moral duty" to fight desires that play havoc with his feelings of inner harmony.

He dreamt of simple human happiness, the blessings of family comfort available to anyone who conforms to convention. Destiny, however, willed it differently.

Tchaikovsky's favorite theme of destiny, which is the keynote of all his large and most brilliant compositions, partly stemmed from his painful private problems. Hence the motifs of struggle against, and triumphs over, destiny; the grief of defeats in a hopeless contest against it powerful forces.

Such ups-and-downs had their reasons: his impassioned love of life sustained his optimistic spirit in the face of adversity. He did not despair under every blow but tried to convince himself that life was worth living after all.

His sadness and heart-rending anguish of loneliness strangely co-existed with a naive implicit faith in the future. His love of life paradoxically generated fear of death. In fact, he had been morbidly afraid of death since boyhood. Two tragic events of that time never loosened their grip on his memory: his mother's early death from cholera and the death of one of his schoolmates from scarlet fever. The unfortunate boy had caught it from the little Tchaikovsky, who was the unwitting germ carrier, though his own life was spared by that deadly scourge of the children of that time.

The composer could never get rid of his guilt feelings about his friend's untimely death.

As years went by, the theme of destiny in his music, which was a reflection on his emotional experiences and impressions of day-to-day life, more and more clearly assumed the philosophical significance of a theme of death. That was a theme of everlasting sleep, torpor and lifelessness, a theme of nothingness, the unconsciousness of non-existence.

The dreadful spectre of death had often haunted him in different periods of his life. Even as a young man he had complained of disillusionment with life, describing it as senseless, selfish and lonely. He had nobody to love and care for. His heart was empty and cold.

That discrepancy between the time-honored conventions of social life and his own calling, between the traditional range of daily duties and the way of life he had to lead constantly pained him and caused friction in his relations with the people he loved and respected.

His father, who was an engineer and a stickler for social conformity, was unable to resign himself to whatever slight digression from the prevailing tenor of social behavior might be committed by his son. He wanted him to be a family man with a flock of children and a steady job.

As a devout Christian believer, who cherished his blood relations with his near and dear ones, the composer was painfully aware of his inadequacy and lived in constant fear of nasty rumors and gossip. He was eager to comply with his father's wish and married, but his marriage was a disaster and only added insult to injury.

He was a constant target of ugly gossip, pointed hints, ridicule and malicious slander, which deprived him of the peace of mind and strained his nerves to a breaking point. The poet Apukhtin, his old time "buddy" of the law school, used to comfort him: "Take it easy. Ignore the stench of public opinion."

In the years following his divorce, however, the composer was unable to put up with the punishment society metes out to whoever is so different from the common

P. I. Tchaikovsky. Circa 1899.

crowd as to deserve any injustice. His suffering was made worse by his awareness of his failure as a husband.

That was a burden on his conscience he could not relieve by any confession. He was secretive and shy to the point of self-humiliation. That was when he attempted to take his life. That seemed the only way to escape the disgrace of defeat.

But now the unexpected happened. Nadezhda von Meck, the wealthy widow of an industrial magnate and reputedly one of the richest women in Europe, came on the scene. She was an ardent admirer of Tchaikovsky's music and probably had a secret flame for the young composer.

Aware of his financial difficulties, she persuaded Tchaikovsky to accept an annuity from her.

"Wealth has no meaning unless it helps genius", she argued in a letter to the embarrassed composer.

That was a chance for him to travel abroad, and he seized it, albeit after some hesitation. He was eager to escape from the daily routine that had swamped him. That was, in fact, a flight from reality.

From the viewpoint of "normal" people, such as his father, Tchaikovsky was leading a dissolute life. He travelled from country to country, from town to town, without a definite aim, a stable income, or his own home stocked with all the attributes of comfortable living.

His life was, indeed, irregular and devoid of stability and a clear purpose, but only on the face of it. The conviction that music alone would give vent to his pent-up emotions and a meaning to his life was steadily growing in his mind.

Music was a bridge to eternity and a way towards a triumph over the unfair destiny. As his awareness of his supreme destination grew clearer, the theme of destiny assumed an ever more generalized philosophical message in his music. Like Gherman in THE QUEEN OF SPADES he defied not only his own destiny and nature but challenged Death herself, the fatal forces denying Man his birthright to freedom and happiness.

The agonizing inner conflict, however, was relentlessly taking its toll and finally erupted in another emotional crisis as his life was drawing to its end. That crisis was all the more painful on the background of his general success.

His life was headed for catastrophe, and his vision of it contrasted paradoxically with his public triumphs as a genius of music. He preserved outward calm, and nothing in his manner betrayed his rising emotional tension.

He even bought a house in the small town of Klin outside Moscow, showing his intention to settle in Russia for good. The high society of the imperial capital St. Petersburg lavished praises upon him.

Nevertheless, the anticipation of doom that had seized hold of him made him feel helpless and lonely. Destiny was knocking on his door, inviting him to play the last act of the great drama of life.

A Farewell to Life

Some of Tchaikovsky's contemporaries in their reminiscences of his last days testify that death was the last thing he expected. He brimmed with energy, feeling younger than his age, and his head was full of creative plans. Death snuffed out his life suddenly when he seemed to be happy as a bird, and not only with his music.

Was that really so?

In his last photos Tchaikovsky looks a tired old man, his pinched face worn by suffering and passions. However, he was only 53 when he died. This image of a man "hoary with age", as his friend H. Laroche, a music critic, remarked once, could hardly belong to one fully satisfied with life, a musician who had chosen Apukhtin's "Requiem" for the secret program of his Sixth Symphony.

That was a supplication to a deity for a rest in peace for one sinful and guilty, interspersed with vague allusions to the jealousy and slander of enemies and ill-wishers that had ruined the life of the lyrical hero. It was pervaded with mystical fear of the Last Judgment and anguish from an awareness that those he loved would turn their backs on him at the crucial moment when he needed them most.

True, his success with the public and his better living added a degree of tranquility to the last years of his life, at least outwardly. His daily life was now more orderly and reasonably planned to leave enough time for composition. Whatever was mundane and petty did not distract him any longer.

The shadow of death, however, was hovering above him. His friends and relatives died one after another. Within two or three years he lost almost all of those he loved. The death of his darling sister Alexandra, his "guardian angel and fairy Ondine", as he called her, was a terrible shock.

News of her death reached him when he was composing the "Kingdom of Sweets" for The Nutcracker. Tchaikovsky made a piano duet arrangement of the ballet for her son Vladimir Davydov and dedicated the Sixth Symphony to him.

The death of the poet Apukhtin, his long-time friend and a constant source of encouragement, was another severe blow. The poet, who was of the same age as the composer, had departed a few months before Tchaikovsky's death.

The noose of death was tightening around his neck. He felt helpless and unable to break its relentless grip.

The rupture with Nadezhda von Meck shortly before he had completed *The Nutcracker* seemed to be an inevitable link in the chain of tragic events. He felt insulted by that sudden breach of long friendship. His wealthy patroness's attentions to him had probably antagonized her adult children, so she had chosen to sacrifice relations with the composer to the interests of accord within her family.

Tchaikovsky was a tragic composer who had experienced the tragedy of life in the vulgar society of imperial Russia with its worship of private wealth and its deaf and dumb public opinion. In the phrase of the great Russian poet Alexander Blok, that was a period of "deaf years".

The imperial grandeur of the semi-feudal state, the arrogant stupidity of the aristocracy, and the vegetable existense of the petty bourgeois created a stifling social climate. Growing public discontent exploded in a wave of senseless terrorism which led the country into a moral and political deadlock.

The Sixth Symphony was a funeral tool for the genius of Russian music crushed by the despotic system of the imperial state. It was also a knell for a whole century of Russian history, a century started by the heinous crime of patricide (assassination of Emperor Paul I in a coup d'etat led by his son Alexander) and now ending amidst the blood and tears of the impoverished peasants.

The Nutcracker was a sweet dream of the golden age of childhood. It was an appeal for rescue without a hint of despair, a reminiscence of blissful days linking the past gone forever, with the present fading out of the dying mind. Fear and hope were blended in a farewell to life.

The Chronicle

Tchaikovsky wrote *The Nutcracker* in record time: he had started work on the music in mid-February 1891 and had completed it, in fact, towards the end of June. Of the four months he spent on this work the periods from March 6 to 31 and from April 5 to the end of May should be excluded. The composer was busy with other work at the time. In fact, he composed the ballet in a mere two months.

The sequence of events linked with his work on *The Nutcracker* is presented below in chronological order.

November-December 1890. The first negotiations with the Directorate of the Russian Imperial Theatres for writing a ballet and opera for a composite production.

"I have been requested to write a one-act opera and a two-act ballet. Vsevolozhsky favors me more and more, saying that a season without my new composition is unthinkable" (excerpt from Tchaikovsky's letter of December 24, 1890).

January 22, 1891. In a letter to his brother Anatole the composer informs him of his new trip to St. Petersburg for the final talks (at the time Tchaikovsky lived either at the Grand Hotel in the central quarter of Moscow or at Frolovskoye in the city's environs where he rented a cottage).

The end of January-February 11. Tchaikovsky stays in St. Petersburg. On February 5 the choreographer Marius Petipa submits to the composer the stage plan of the first act of *The Nutcracker.*

February 12 to 18. Tchaikovsky begins his work on the ballet. By all indications prior to the final talks the composer had an ambivalent attitude to its subject. *"...I am beginning to reconcile myself to the ballet plot"*, he writes in a letter to his brother Modest the day before his decisive visit to St. Petersburg.

By February 18 Tchaikovsky had already composed the first two numbers of the ballet and most of the dances for the national divertissement initially planned for the first act.

February 18 to 21. Tchaikovsky makes another trip to St. Petersburg to meet with Vsevolozhsky, who informs the composer that the divertissement will be expunged from the first act.

February 22. Upon his return to Frolovskoye from St. Petersburg Tchaikovsky begins to compose the entrée and scene of Godfather Drosselmeier.

February 23. Tchaikovsky's friend Jurgensen sends to Frolovskoye a crate with children's musical instruments and sheet music the composer needs for writing the ballet.

The author's manuscript of the ballet score contains numerous remarks indicating where and how these instruments should be used. Tchaikovsky attached great significance to them, seeking to create a very distinctive atmosphere of action.

From February 22 to March 6 the composer intensively worked on the ballet. True, there was a measure of inconsistency in his composition. In the first act he skipped the dance of the parents and guests, the scene of the ballet between the mice and the toy soldiers, and changed over to the "Waltz of Snowflakes" immediately after the episodes with Drosselmeier.

March 6. Tchaikovsky leaves St. Petersburg for Paris. On the day of his departure he has a meeting with Petipa to discuss the stage plan of the second act that will be sent to his Paris address on March 9.

March 6 to 31. Tchaikovsky's work on the ballet has come to a standstill but, as evidenced by surviving documents, he is simply taking his time and bracing up for another big effort to complete it as soon as possible.

"I will try to work during my sea journey (to America). Even on my way here I did some composing by fits and starts" (excerpt from a letter of March 8 he sent from Berlin).

March 10. Tchaikovsky arrives in Paris. It proved impossible for the composer to work on the ballet in Paris. In a letter to his nephew Vladimir Davydov he complains: *"I don't know where to go to be able to concentrate on the ballet."*

March 31. Tchaikovsky moves to Rouen in northern France where he works without a respite on sketches for *The Nutcracker* until his sailing off for the United States on April 5.

April 3. Tchaikovsky informs Vsevolozhsky in a letter that the first act will be ready in two days. He also requests a period of grace, since he is unable to meet the deadline. The reason was not his alleged discontent with the libretto but his fatigue after many days of over-exertion and, most important of all, his futile attempts to cope with the second act which he considered crucial to the ballet.

He wrote to Vsevolozhsky: *"I have yet to perform a very daring musical trick...The second act can be made extremely fascinating, but this requires filigree work, for which I have no time enough and, what matters most, no predisposition to inspired work...*

"I tried to do my level best but I tried in vain. My efforts came to nothing ," he confessed in a letter to his brother Modest.

In such situations Tchaikovsky usually felt disgust for the work he was composing. The Nutcracker and even King Rene's Daughter (Iolanta) "turned into nightmares so hateful as to defy description". He wrote to Vsevolozhsky: "These images give me no joy or inspiration; they terrify and haunt me day and night..."

That was, in effect, a normal crisis of self-confidence visiting a creative mind. In the same letter to Vsevolozhsky the composer assured him that if he were granted a grace and rested awhile he would certainly come up with two masterpieces of music (an opera and a ballet).

April 5. Tchaikovsky's crisis is made worse by his sister's death of which he learns by chance from a newspaper. He writes in a letter to his brother Modest: "I am knocked out and unable to compose the Kingdom of Sweets, a travel to which makes the second act of the ballet."

April 7. Vsevolozhsky, who understands the composer's problem, writes in a letter to him: "We would rather wait for a year than force you to write operas and ballets without any desire or inspiration."

May 9. Tchaikovsky leaves the United States.

May 20. He returns to St. Petersburg and immediately proceeds to Maidanovo.

June 2. Tchaikovsky's work on the ballet is in full swing. *"I have got down to work, and it is going on without a hitch"*, he writes to the composer M.M. Ippolitov-Ivanov.

June 3. Tchaikovsky informs Jurgensen that he is composing the second act and requests him to buy a celesta, a new musical instrument with an angelic voice. He asks Jurgensen to keep it a secret lest some of his rivals, particularly Rimsky-Korsakov, get wind of his intentions.

The celesta was bought abroad and brought to Russia with full precautions. Tchaikovsky used it for the female variations in the second act of *The Nutcracker*.

June 3 to 24. The composition of the ballet enters its final stage. Tchaikovsky writes to his nephew Vladimir Davydov that his new work is indisputably successful. *"The time is not up yet and I can do more,"* he tells him in the same letter.

June 24. Tchaikovsky's work on the ballet is over.

June 25. *"The ballet is worthless compared with 'The Sleeping Beauty'. This is clear as daylight to me"*, he suddenly admits in a letter to his nephew.

June 27. *"I am haunted by doubts about my fitness now that I have finished the ballet score in the rough"*, Tchaikovsky says in a letter to his favorite pupil Sergei Taneyev, a pianist and composer who was requested to make a piano arrangement of *The Nutcracker*.

January 1 to March 23, 1892. At Maidanovo, Tchaikovsky orchestrates the ballet, making up an orchestral suite of individual numbers. The suite had been performed in concerts before *The Nutcracker* was staged.

March 7. The first performance of the suite from *The Nutcracker* at a concert of the Russian Musical Society conducted by Tchaikovsky.

December 6. The ballet and the opera *Iolanta* have their first night at the Marinsky Opera House in St. Petersburg.

Tchaikovsky's Work Habits

This may be of interest to ballet and music lovers. Tchaikovsky's work routine was unusual and anticipated in a way the style of work of modern composers.

He composed music practically every day. He had no faith in the mystical power of inspiration and regarded those who reposed their hopes in it as dabblers.

His steady efforts, it is true, sometimes resulted in nervous tension, as was the case, for instance, in the Rouen period of composing *The Nutcracker*. He often had to struggle with his apathy and fatigue and what he called "a reluctance to compose".

On the whole, however, he followed the rules of work he had set for himself with hairsplitting diligence. He had trained himself to compose music continuously and in any situation regardless of the prevailing circumstances.

"I can say that I invent music every instant of my life in whatever surroundings. At times I seem to observe with curiosity the endless work going on in the musical area of my brain irrespective of the subject I may be discussing with other persons".

Tchaikovsky had implicit faith in hard work. *"One must be patient and dedicated, and inspiration will inevitably visit one who has been able to overcome his revulsion to work."*

New ideas often entered his head unexpectedly. He did not know how and why and called that an *"impenetrable mystery"*. The famous theme of the adagio of the Sixth Symphony sprang up in his mind so suddenly that he put it down on a hotel bill, the first scrap of paper that was at hand.

He loved to work in complete isolation and could not stand the presence of anybody but his servants at home. Setting to work on *The Queen of Spades*, he flatly refused to take his brother Modest with him to Florence, although he needed him as the author of the libretto not yet completed at the time.

When working on his sketches, he used to get up at eight in the morning, sat down to his desk at nine, made a break from one to five o'clock in the afternoon, then worked until seven o'clock in the evening, which was the knocking-off time. Then he could mingle with friends and acquaintances.

Tchaikovsky's tremendous powers of work were surrounded with legends already in his lifetime.

He wrote his sketches in bound notebooks of varying sizes. *The Nutcracker* occupies one half of the three notebooks of 86, 92 and 102 pages containing the opera *Iolanta* and the ballet. All the sketches are made with a soft black pencil for added facility in writing.

Eugene Hunst, a student of Tchaikovsky's methods of composition, writes that he never numbered the pages of his sketches but wrote the names of his friends to guide him in case he needed to locate the relevant passage. He wrote, for instance: *See Taneyev* . Some of his references are amusing. One of them reads: *See the cab-driver.*

Tchaikovsky was a stickler for accuracy. He invariably marked the date of beginning a composition on his sketches and sometimes indicated where and when a musical idea had crossed his mind. In his sketches of *The Nutcracker*, for example, he indicated that he had invented the coda when *"taking a walk in St. Petersburg"*.

This tragic portrait was made at the time of the first performance of *The Nutcracker* in 1893. Tchaikovsky died a few weeks after the performance from a sudden and very mysterious ailment. Rumor has it that he was forced to commit suicide when his homosexual relationship with his nephew was discovered.

The sketches of his last years bear his constant appeals to God. On the title page of his sketches for *The Nutcracker* we can read: *"God Almighty, to thy mercy I submit myself."*

Every movement of the Sixth Symphony ends in words of gratitude to God.

The composer never made any drafts except sketches. Once a sketch was complete, he immediately went over to orchestration. As Hunst testifies, *"Tchaikovsky's sketches present a full scheme of the orchestral score"*.

The composer thought in terms of an orchestra. He imagined and heard a composition in his mind as if it were complete. He said in a letter to Nadezhda von Meck in 1878 that a musical idea was born in his mind simultaneously with its orchestration.

Therefore, Tchaikovsky's sketches brought to perfection in every detail seemed to be sounding on paper and were a meticulous prototype of the future score.

In the process of orchestration he simply deciphered a sketch. He did that with skilful ease, nothing could distract him from this work which was a pleasure to him and kept him in a cheerful mood. He considered a composition complete as soon as he was through with its sketches.

Thus, *The Nutcracker* had actually been finished precisely on June 24, 1891.

The True Librettist and Petipa

The name of the librettist of *The Nutcracker* displayed on its modern bills is Marius Petipa. This is a mistake. History has been unfair to the true author of the libretto, who was the initiator of the request for the ballet and its stage production. His name is Ivan Vsevolozhsky.

In fact, on the bills of the première of 1892 Vsevolozhsky figured as the librettist, while Petipa was named as the author of the ballet programme, which was news not only to the Russian ballet theatre. Why this happened at all is the subject of further story. Petipa had played an intricate part in the preparation of the first production of *The Nutcracker*.

Vsevolozhsky was a well-educated man with a good knowledge of literature. He also had a record of experience in writing ballet scenarios. The libretto of *The Sleeping Beauty* was of his penmanship. This fact is not called in question by anybody.

Petipa had really made sketches of the libretto of *The Nutcracker*. By all indications, however, he had never read E.T.A. Hoffmann's fairy tale and most likely followed a lead given him by someone familiar with it. Hence all of his tentative sketches of the libretto were widely discrepant with the Hoffmann story.

In a letter to Laroche, Modest Tchaikovsky told him that he had recounted the literary plot of the ballet from what he had heard from Vsevolozhsky. In fact, he had simply written down the Director's libretto, which gave Petipa the guidelines for his plan of stage action. The original libretto which has survived to date is well written and shows its author's very good knowledge of Hoffmann's tale. Petipa had received it from Vsevolozhsky in January, 1891.

Petipa's plan is a unique document which has not yet lost its value for professionals.

The choreographer had first used this method of collaboration with the composer in the production of *The Sleeping Beauty*. That was a perfectly new form of relationship between the theatre and the composer. Already the plan of *The Sleeping Beauty* Tchaikovsky has used to write the score had indicated exactly the time, duration and character of every number. The plan laid down the scheme of the future production.

The success of *The Sleeping Beauty* had confirmed the effectiveness of the new method. *The Nutcracker* was provided with a similar plan for musical action and dance.

Just as in the case of *The Sleeping Beauty* Petipa drew up the plan of *The Nutcracker* in minute detail. Here is a fragment of the second scene of his plan.

Choreographer
Yuri Grigorovich

Choreographer
Marius Petipa

Choreographer
Lev Ivanov

Choreographer
Alexander Gorsky

Designer
Simon Virsaladze

"No. 19. The stage is vacant. It is nighttime. Moonlight flows into the sitting-room through a window. Eight bars of gentle and mysterious music.

"Clara (Marie's name in the ballet) dressed in a night gown cautiously comes back. She is eager to see her precious sick toy before going to bed. Another eight bars of even more mysterious music for her entrée. She feels scared. Two bars to show her shivering with fright. She comes up to the Nutcracker's bed, which seems to be emitting fantastic glow. Eight bars of fantastic and mysterious music.

"The clock strikes midnight. A pause for music. Clara looks up and, to her alarm, sees Drosselmeier sitting on top of the clock and grinning at her ironically. She tries to run away but her legs would not carry her. There is a tremolo. The chime of the clock is followed by another short tremolo to express her terror.

"No. 20. In the silence of night she hears the scuffling of mice. She makes an effort to move but is surrounded by mice on all sides. The tremolo is followed by four bars to imitate the scuffling of mice and another four bars expressing their squealing and squeaking. Gripped by terror Clara flinches back and tries to take the unfortunate Nutcracker and escape. She is so frightened, however, that her strength wanes and she helplessly sinks into a chair. The mice scuttle away. Their squealing is followed by eight bars at a rapid tempo ending in a chord (when she sinks into the chair).

"No. 21. The Christmas Tree grows enormously large. Forty-eight bars of fantastic music with a grandiose crescendo.

"No. 22. The sentry on duty shouts: **"Freeze! Identify yourself!"** Three bars. This is followed by two bars of silence. The sentry fires. One or two bars. The dolls are in panic. Two bars of terror. The sentry has awakened the hare drummers. Eight bars for awakening and eight bars for the alarm signal, then four to eight bars for drawing up ranks. The battle of 48 bars. During the battle the dolls climb down the fir tree and start preparing lint for the wounded soldiers. The mice are advancing and eating up gingerbread men. Eight bars after forty-eight bars of the battle to make one hear how the mice are gnawing gingerbread.

"No. 23. The Mouse King makes his appearance. His army loudly welcomes him. His entrée is accompanied by shrill vicious music offending the ear. This is followed by a battle cry: '**Squeak! Squeak!**' (**Hurray!**). *Eight bars for the Mouse King's entrée and four bars for the shouts of hurray (***Squeak! Squeak!***)*.

"*No. 24. The Nutcracker calls on his old guard shouting* '**To arms!**' *Four bars and eight bars for battle formation.*"

Signed *Marius Petipa*

It is obvious that the libretto had been made by someone thoroughly familiar with Hoffmann's tale, and Petipa spelt it out in forms clear and convenient to the composer. Without revising the content and idea of every number Petipa only specified its place in the general composition and briefly outlined the character of each scene.

Later Petipa used the same system in his work on Glazunov's *Raymonda*. Today almost all choreographers apply this method pioneered by Petipa.

Tchaikovsky and Hoffmann

Preparing his piano arrangement of *The Nutcracker* for publication, Tchaikovsky wrote on the title page that the subject of the ballet had been borrowed from Hoffmann's and Dumas père's fairy tales.

His publisher Jurgensen resolutely objected to that. He said in a letter to the composer that his reference to Dumas père was irrelevant, because the latter was not the original author of the fairy tale. Moreover, he had only recently died, and his heirs might claim copyright for the libretto.

Jurgensen was apprehensive of a possible law suit. He was also correct in essence. "I know Hoffmann's fairy tale very well. In fact, I have it in my library," he wrote.

Tchaikovsky agreed with his arguments and deleted the name of Dumas père from his manuscript. One may wonder why he had originally insisted on including the name of the famous French novelist. Indeed, the latter had simply translated Hoffmann's tale into French.

The French translation of Hoffmann's fairy tale Tchaikovsky had read in Florence contained only a part of *The Nutcracker's* story before the adventures of Marie who fell in love with her wooden toy.

In Hoffmann's fairy tale, Godfather Drosselmeier who had given Marie the mysterious Nutcracker as a Christmas present, tells her the story of a handsome young man turned by witchcraft into an ugly wooden toy pursued by the vindictive Mouse King.

The Tale of the Hard Nut is the name of this story in Hoffmann's fairy tale. Drosselmeier's young nephew releases Princess Pirlipat from the spell of witchcraft by which the powerful Mistress Mousie, the mother of the Mouse King, turned her into an ugly doll. The Princess becomes young and beautiful again, but the young man turns into an ugly Nutcracker toy. The ungrateful Princess rejects him. He lives a miserable life but he can become a prince and a king if he could break the spell by defeating the seven-headed Mouse King and if he could find a lady to love him in spite of his ugliness.

Dumas père had translated *The Tale of the Hard Nut* . The story of Marie, the heroine of Hoffmann's tale, offered to the composer as a ballet subject was absent in the translation.

Tchaikovsky was probably surprised, reading the outline of the libretto of the future ballet in December, 1890. Dumas père's *"Princess Pirlipat and the Nutcracker"* he had read in Florence was different from the story of a certain Clara (as Marie was renamed in the libretto by Vsevolozhsky and Petipa) who travels with the Nutcracker to the Kingdom of Sweets.

One may wonder whether Tchaikovsky was really unfamiliar with Hoffmann's fairy tale either in the original or in some full translation.

Strictly speaking, no direct evidence to this effect is available. Moveover, there is a reason to suppose that Tchaikovsky had a dim idea of Hoffmann's works in general.

In the entire vast literary heritage of the composer---his letters, diaries, articles and notes---Hoffmann is never mentioned, although Tchaikovsky liked to discuss his impressions of what he read with his friends and relatives. It is significant that even Hoffmann's opera on the subject of Ondine, in which Tchaikovsky took a lively interest as long as he lived, was never mentioned by him. He was most likely unaware of its existence, probably because its score had long been listed as missing and had in fact been forgotton towards the middle of the last century.

But the most eloquent argument in favor of the view that Hoffmann was practically unknown to Tchaikovsky is to be found in his correspondence with Jurgensen in the 1880's.

Discussing with him the title of a suite on a theme of Mozart he had just completed, the composer expressed his apprehensions lest the title *Mozartiana* that he liked should evoke undesirable mental associations with Schumann's widely known *Kreisleriana*.

Tchaikovsky hated imitation, even in titles, and was confident that Schumann's *Kreisleriana* was named after the musician and composer Kreisler who had lived in the first half of the 19th century.

Schumann, however, had meant a different Kreisler as Tchaikovsky learned from Jurgensen! *Kreisleriana* derived its name from Johannes Kreisler, the hero of Hoffmann's literary works.

There was a spiritual affinity between Tchaikovsky and Hoffmann. Both idolized Mozart as an ideal in music and held similar views on art and the artist's destination. In his young years Tchaikovsky had been under the powerful influence of Schumann, the author of the musical "Hoffmanniads", though he was unaware of that. Tchaikovsky had subconsciously absorbed Hoffmann's ideas and fantasy.

Vsevolozhsky Versus Petipa

Vsevolozhsky borrowed the idea of a composite ballet and opera production from the experience of French opera. As the Director of the Russian Imperial Theatres he was always on the look-out for new forms of theatrical presentation.

Vsevolozhsky sought to revise the traditions of a large-scale fairy ballet, of which *The Sleeping Beauty*, staged but recently, was an ideal specimen. He wanted a more entertaining and piquant performance with unexpected twists and turns. Long before Fokine and Diaghilev, he had realized the danger of routine in which the Russian ballet, led by its patriarch Marius Petipa, was gradually bogging down.

Therefore, he reposed great hopes in *The Nutcracker*, which was to give new life to the art of the Marinsky ballet. Tchaikovsky took a favorable view of his idea, as it allowed him to give free rein to his imagination. In fact, the score of *The Nutcracker* in its final form is a "capriccio" of its own kind, fancifully irregular in form.

Petipa, however, was of a different mind. His conflict with Vsevolozhsky had begun at the stage of making the scenario and came into the open after the end of negotiations with Tchaikovsky when Petipa gave him his plan of the first act.

In a letter to Tchaikovsky, Vsevolozhsky accused Petipa of conservatism.

"He is what the French call vieux genre (old genre). The solo and all variations he has invented for the first act would be uninteresting to the public."

Vsevolozhsky took direction of the production into his own hands. Significantly, transferring the dances of the divertissement from the first to the second act, Tchaikovsky ignored Petipa and tersely stated: *"'Vsevolozhsky wants no dances here."*

At first glance, the conflict between Vsevolozhsky and Petipa arose from this divertissement, but actually it had deeper roots and threw into salient relief the wide difference between their general principles. In the same letter to Tchaikovsky, Vsev-

This is a very rare sketch of Tchaikovsky when he was a young man of 23 years of age. Because it was unsigned, it is quite possible that the sketch was made in his later life.

olozhsky angrily remarked that *"variations of all these Mademoiselles Johannsons, Zhukovas and Nedromskayas (dancers of the Marinsky ballet) are a bore to the greater part of the audience."* The Director was evidently referring to *The Sleeping Beauty* in Petipa's choreography, which abounded in female variations.

Vsevolozhsky detested repetition and was unwilling to follow the trodden path of *The Sleeping Beauty*. On the contrary, Petipa was bent on trying again what had once brought him success.

Petipa visualized *The Nutcracker* as a grand ballet in his own style, that is, a performance with large dance ensembles (of the type of the grand pas "Shadows" in *La Bayadere* or "Nereids" in *The Sleeping Beauty*), magnificent divertissements, and complex choreographic compositions at places irrelevant to the development of the action.

For his part, Vsevolozhsky planned a ballet with none of these components. In his opinion, the divertissement in the first act would only slow down the action and lend it undue significance and pomposity.

Vsevolozhsky's imagination was of an impressionist stamp as compared with Petipa's classical academicism. The Director wanted to stage a playful ballet with tin soldiers popping out of their boxes and a succession of laconic sketches conveying serious ideas in jocular form. Vsevolozhsky visualized these scenes of childhood as a mischievous puppet show serious in meaning but comically exaggerated from the viewpoint of an adult spectator.

Vsevolozhsky was sensitive to the winds of change. In contrast to Petipa who still confined himself to his favorite theme of amorous gallantry, Vsevolozhsky caught sight of a new theme coming into fashion, the theme of a puppet.

The theme of puppets in ballet offered new opportunities in the genre of comedy, presenting a new type of mechanical movements with various comical effects. This new trend in stage art had a reverse side. A toy that was a plaything of history showed the social collisions of real life. The voice of a vulnerable and defenseless soul appealed for sympathy from the stage. It was not fortuitous that *The Nutcracker* became the forerunner of Igor Stravinsky's tragic *Petrouchka*.

On the eve of the rehearsals of the ballet Petipa was taken ill. Then he had to look after his sick daughter and dropped out of the production.

The production was entrusted to Lev Ivanov, the second choreographer of the Marinsky Theatre and Petipa's invariable assistant. Petipa allowed his name to be left on the bills as the author of the ballet programme. In the event of success Petipa would be hailed as the brilliant master of choreography and in the event of failure Lev Ivanov would be the scapegoat.

Indeed, critics that berated the première blamed Lev Ivanov for his alleged incompetence and expressed their regrets about the absence of Petipa, who would certainly have achieved superlative results. They were unaware that Petipa had never intended to stage *The Nutcracker*. After the triumph of *The Sleeping Beauty* he was apprehensive of any risk of failure. And he was confident that direction of that innovative ballet would put at risk his faultless reputation.

Lev Ivanov and the Première

Lev Ivanov was a diffident and self-effacing man, unhappy in family life, who worked hard in the shadow of the great Petipa, never claiming a share of the latter's fame. Petipa regarded Ivan, as he called Ivanov, as his hired hand and used him to his own advantage.

Ivanov worshipped Petipa and was fearful of higher authority. Even in his heart of hearts he did not dream of winning a comparable position, although potentially he was a genius of choreography, by no means inferior to Petipa. However, he lacked

determination and the necessary strength of character and preferred to take orders from his illustrious maestro.

It would seem that the right to an independent production of *The Nutcracker*, a ballet by Russia's finest composer, that was to be the hit of the season was the chance of a lifetime for Ivanov. He was not ambitious, however. The trust of the Directorate did not encourage him but faced him with the problem of survival. He regarded his honorable assignment as a risky venture.

Vsevolozhsky certainly knew of Ivanov's failings but admired his musicality and near professional skill in playing the piano. Vsevolozhsky had missed a different point, the fact that Ivanov had a profoundly lyrical turn of mind. Small wonder, therefore, that three years later he would become the author of the swan scenes in Tchaikovsky's *Swan Lake*, which were perhaps the most significant event in the history of the Russian ballet.

The music of *The Nutcracker* held out different opportunities for a choreographer. Ivanov could hardly feel its humorous intonations, subtle irony, and charming ambiguity captivating the listener with its understatement.

To make matters worse, though he was formally allowed to handle the production on his own, Ivanov had Petipa's plan on his hands and was expected to comply with it to a T. Ivanov was too shy to try to make corrections in it. On top of everything, he was hard pressed for time, but Vsevolozhsky would not listen to any talk about extending the deadline. The ballet, prepared in an atmosphere of confusion and haste, had its first night on schedule

After the première Tchaikovsky informed his brother Modest that *"the opera and ballet were a great success. The opera seemed to please everybody."*

Two months later, however, he gave a more cautious appraisal of the première: *"It was not an unconditional success. The opera was really admired by all but the ballet was not. For all its splendor it was rather monotonous."*

As evidenced by Akim Volynsky, a leading Russian music critic and historian, at the première of *The Nutcracker*, Tchaikovsky looked happy. After the performance he came on the stage, hugged Ivanov and kissed him on both cheeks.

If Tchaikovsky was partly displeased with the production, he never showed his discontent. Though he was usually sensitive to press criticism, this time he was rather indifferent even to the most vicious attacks against the new ballet. He was confident of his art and drew encouragement from the success of the first public performance of his *Nutcracker* suite.

Reviewers, however, fumed about what they called a puppet show, which was unworthy of the Marinsky Theatre and insulting to the exquisite taste of true ballet lovers. The new Director of Imperial Theatres, Telyakovsky, remarked caustically that the costumes and stage scenery of *The Nutcracker* looked like a display of sweetmeats in a confectioner's shop.

What were the reasons for Ivanov's setback and what problems he proved unable to cope with in conveying the message of Tchaikovsky's music?

In keeping with Tchaikovsky's conception and Petipa's plan of stage action the main characters in the ballet were children. Their parts were danced by ballet school pupils.

That was in agreement with the plot. Neither Vsevolozhsky nor Petipa, however, realized clearly the difficulties involved in organizing a ballet production with dancers whose inadequate technique was a handicap to the choreographer's fantasy. Sophisticated forms of dance were impossible here, although the music demanded them for all its outward simplicity.

A scene from the First Act of *The Nutcracker* taken during the opening night in the Marinsky Theatre in St. Petersburg, 1892.

That was especially true of the second "night scene," of the battle between mice and toy soldiers, the episode of the growth of the Christmas Tree, and the lyrical andante before the *Waltz of Snowflakes*. The choreographer had to rely on pantomime and decorative effects to try to convey the meaning of the music.

This required direction of dramatic action rather than dance, which was beyond the powers of either Ivanov or Petipa. The heroes' story became vague and incoherent and was reduced to a succession of more or less picturesque "confectionery" scenes.

In fact, Ivanov presented a review of favorite children's games and naive dreams, which failed to show the heroes' emotions in the kaleidoscopic change of individual numbers.

As evidenced by Akim Volynsky, Ivanov's best achievement in the ballet was the *Waltz of Snowflakes,* which has unfortunately not survived to date. That was a large dance ensemble, which was choreographic form in which Ivanov was in his element.

Sixty-four dancers formed fantastic compositions resembling patterns of hoar-frost. In the lyrical culminations of the music, Ivanov presented scenes of severe winter nature pervaded with tension and expectations of change. Here he expressed his subtle appreciation of the music, which remained a mystery in the last century.

The Music

In Tchaikovsky's music *The Nutcracker* is linked with the *Children's Album,* a piano cycle he had composed back in 1878, at the end of his Moscow period. In expert opinion, it contains what may be called a summary of the future ballet. In fact, the *Children's Album* could make an independent ballet.

Long before he had composed *The Nutcracker* the images of childhood had obtruded themselves on his mind. As his life was drawing to a close, the composer more and more often came back in thought to the world of his past, as though reliving his life as a child in the cozy family circle under the Christmas Tree, which became the symbol of the tree of knowledge in the ballet.

The Nutcracker story had a hidden meaning to the composer. It was a journey to the abode of his own feelings. His life was reflected in the images of childhood like in a magic mirror.

The heroine falls in love with an ugly toy, which hides a beautiful fairy tale prince. Her life is mysteriously divided between day and night, dreams and reality. Her dormant feelings are awakened by danger to her beloved. The conflict between good and evil ends in the triumph of love. She learns the meaning of life through a contest with death. The *Waltz of Snowflakes* Tchaikovsky wrote for an orchestra and a children's choir is the culmination of the music liberating the heroes from their earthly concerns and raising them to a blissful life of eternity.

This "poem of childhood", as the ballet was called by many Russian musicologists, was Tchaikovsky's confession, a unique lyrical autobiography. In their revived images of the past he sought a way out of his crisis which had doomed him to death. *The Nutcracker* was a sweet dream, the last refuge of a despairing soul.

The 20th Century

In the 20th century the first choreographer to stage *The Nutcracker* was Alexander Gorsky. Raised by the St. Petersburg ballet, he had moved to Moscow at the turn of the century and led the Bolshoi ballet for about twenty years.

He went down in history as a reformer of the strict academic style of dance. Gorsky admired Stanislavsky's reforms at the Moscow Art Theatre and seriously considered the need for applying his sytem to the ballet stage.

Gorsky originated the Moscow school of dance distinctive for its dramatic and dynamic style, freedom of movement, and disregard for academic canons.

Gorsky first produced *The Nutcracker* at the Bolshoi in 1919. Regarding it as a ballet for children, he organized its action in keeping with the canons of the Petipa era, presenting large dance ensembles and extended choreographic scenes. To make it a full-length ballet of interest to adult spectators he rearranged musical numbers into a three-act production instead of the former two acts.

The *Waltz of Snowflakes* was a separate act incorporating the famous adagio from the second act of the score. Following the logic of the plot the first act was devoted to genre scenes and the details of the story. The second act showed the heroine's journey to the *Kingdom of Sweets*. The third act was a dream festival.

That faithful compliance with details did not bring Gorsky any closer to understanding the message of the music. His interpretation was very matter-of-fact and prosaic, devoid of fantasy, humor and depth.

To make the ballet true to life, Gorsky turned Drosselmeier into a respectable old burgher whose wife is wooed by young danglers at the Christmas party. The snowflakes, dressed in fur coats and hats, danced in front of Santa Claus. That was Gorsky's idea of the heroine's fantastic dream after she fell asleep in front of an enormous window covered with patterns of hoarfrost.

It was Gorsky who introduced the motif of fantastic sleep into *The Nutcracker*. It is absent in Hoffmann's fairy tale, Tchaikovsky's music and Ivanov's choreography. This motif was preserved in later productions, including Grigorovich's.

Another innovation in Gorsky's version was the heroine's dance of the adagio (pas de deux in the second act of the score). This was later taken up by all producers of *The Nutcracker*, although the transfer of the adagio and its combination with the *Waltz of Snowflakes* deprived the music of the ballet of its culmination.

In Leningrad

In Leningrad the classical version of *The Nutcracker* was challenged by Fedor Lopukhov. It was the year 1923, and the leading dancers of the Marinsky ballet who had left Russia long before the revolution of 1917 were in fact in emigration. They were joined by those who disliked the revolution. The young republic was yet unable to give generous financial aid to the theatre. In that situation the Marinsky ballet was making heroic efforts to preserve at least some of its great productions.

Fedor Lopukhov was a former schoolmate of Vaclav Jijinsky and had taken part in Anna Pavlova's American tour. An enthusiastic supporter of Michel Fokine's ideas, he had a flair for choreographic composition and a gift for organizing and teaching, although he had proved a failure as a dancer on the St. Petersburg stage.

He was thoroughly familiar with the classical heritage and had a reasonable measure of reverence for Petipa, but his head was full of his own ideas and he searched for ways to renovate the classical traditions and remake ballet along new lines consonant with the revolutionary winds of change.

However, he was wise enough to take a cautious view of the carefree rejection of its time-honored basic principles which was in evidence in the early years of the revolution.

Appointed chief choreographer of the Marinsky ballet, he did much to preserve the classics and the St. Petersburg school of dance inherited from the brilliant past of Russian ballet.

The Nutcracker, however, was a different case. Lopukhov intensely disliked Ivanov's version and revised much of it, even the *Waltz of Snowflakes*. He explained that by a shortage of dancers at the time and in later years insisted that Ivanov's waltz was not as good as generally believed and did not rule out other versions.

It may be relevant to recall here that Lopukhov's waltz was forgotten after five years, whereas Ivanov's version lived on for over thirty years and is remembered as a beautiful legend.

In 1923, however, Lopukhov's attack on *The Nutcracker* was still confined to particulars and had not yet gained momentum. Much of Ivanov's version had survived. Incidentally, the *Dance of Buffoons* he had choreographed was brilliantly performed in Lopukhov's production by George Balanchivadze, a young graduate of the St. Petersburg ballet school, who would in time become known to the world as George Balanchine.

The 1923 production of *The Nutcracker* brought no satisfaction to Lopukhov. In 1927 he tried a synthesis of classical dance with acrobatics and athletics in *The Ice*

Maiden to Edvard Grieg's music arranged for ballet by Boris Asafiev, a leading musicologist and composer, who took a keen interest in *The Nutcracker* as long as he lived. He probably encouraged Lopukhov to further experiments with *The Nutcracker*.

The Ice Maiden boosted Lopukhov's ambitions and now that he had gained command of a new dance language he resolved to give battle to the classical version of *The Nutcracker* in 1929.

The result was a far cry from what he had expected. The new version infuriated both the conservatives and the innovators and was dropped from the repertoire immediately after the première. Nothing like that had ever been seen on the stage of the academic theatre, not to speak of the later time.

On the eve of the première Lopukhov was unusually loquacious. He readily granted interviews to newspapermen, explaining the principles of his new production. *"Dance in words, dance without music, integration of dance into acrobatics and grotesque, a search for colors consonant with the tonalities of the music."* That was a spate of innovations he had in store for the unfortunate *Nutcracker*.

He called for a return to Hoffmann's story but loudly proclaimed: *"No miracles!"* This implied that the ballet would be performed by modern actors determined to emphasize its realism.

In the prologue an actress playing the part of *The Nutcracker* climbed through a keyhole depicted in the stage scenery and announced: *"Hi! I'm the Nutcracker!"* In the finale the actors explained to the audience that the ballet was a joke modern actors played on modern spectators.

Lopukhov had concluded for some reason that *The Nutcracker* provided good stuff for social satire and staged it as a revue lampooning human types of imperial Russia. There was a general in epaulettes, a tzar and a tzarina who were the heroine's parents, an official carrying a briefcase, a maid of honor and other hangovers of the despicable past. *The Nutcracker* himself spurned by Princess Pirlipat was almost a victim of social injustice.

In the final lyrical waltz the dancers were riding bicycles. In the pas de deux the heroine was carried to the stage with her head hanging to the floor and her legs resting on her partner's shoulders. Her adagio was a series of acrobatic stunts. The snowflakes were dressed as show girls and performed somersaults. The sick Nutcracker hobbled over the stage on crutches and packed his suitcases in panic to escape from the Mouse King, and the heroine's wedding dress was made of the skin of a defeated mouse.

The shock of the production was so severe that *The Nutcracker* vanished from the ballet stage for a good five years.

Vainonen

The Nutcracker was returned to the ballet stage by Vasily Vainonen. His version was the only one at all of the country's theatres for over thirty years.

His production was devoid of innovative ideas and philosophic sophistication and stirred no feelings of resentment or delight. Nobody objected to it or admired it very much. Critics at first reproached Vainonen for his too prosaic interpretation of Tchaikovsky's music, but little by little resigned themselves to it. The ballet stayed in the repertoire and enjoyed moderate success, while new choreographers brave enough to handle *The Nutcracker* were yet to come.

In time Vainonen's version gradually lost its attraction to adult audiences and became a ballet for children and then was adopted as a school production, occasionally appearing at large theatres.

The finest scene in his version was the *Waltz of Snowflakes*, probably a modernized revival of Ivanov's masterpiece collected from fragments which had survived in the 1923 production of Lopukhov.

In Soviet ballet the 'thirties were a period of asserting the genre of dramatic ballet, which attached first priority to lifelikeness and allowed phantasmagoria only as a fairy tale deserving no more than casual attention in a situation of epoch-making social transformations called upon to make beautiful dreams come true.

Therefore, Vainonen's story of Masha, which was the heroine's name in *The Nutcracker*, contained nothing unusual. There was no conflict between dreams and reality. The girl simply fell asleep in her cosy bed and awakened in the finale. She had a beautiful dream which would come true if she tried hard to help herself. She did it and a happy future opened before her. The message of the ballet addressed to the children was simple: *where there's a will, there's a way.*

In 1939 Vainonen staged *The Nutcracker* at the Bolshoi. It differed but little from what he had produced in Leningrad, but as his last ballet it indisputably proved useful to many brilliant dancers of the future. They performed in it during their years at school or at graduation exams. It was the starting point of their steep rise to fame.

In the 'forties and 'fifties *The Nutcracker* was rated far below other classical ballets. Great dancers did not stay long in its casts, because the ballet could not add much to their fame which they won in *Swan Lake* or in *Giselle* or in monumental dramatic ballets. Reviewing the history of *The Nutcracker* before 1966, we can see that it was often dropped from the repertoire and like its main hero endured many sad experiences.

Grigorovich

At the time when Tchaikovsky read Hoffmann's fairy tale in Florence in the early 1880's, an Italian horse breeder and trainer, a man of noble descent traceable to Dante, lived in the city. His name was Alfredo Rosai, and he was a very knowledgeable man in his field.

In the mid-1880's Alfredo Rosai was invited to Russia by the Duke of Lichtenberg to take charge of his thoroughbred horses. That was a tempting job offer and after some hesitation he resettled in Russia where he soon married a plain peasant woman who bore him three children. The Rosai family lived in St. Petersburg and in the small town of Peterhof, the summer residence of the Russian Tzars.

Alfredo Rosai was highly regarded by his colleagues and was a good family man. In his line of business he made friends with famous circus riders, Truzzi in particular. He was a relative of the famous circus dynasty of Cinzelli, also an Italian by birth.

Strange as it may seem, it was the circus that kindled an interest in ballet within the Rosai family. Ballet also required high professional skill, filigree technique and an impeccably plastic body.

Alfredo's eldest son Georgy Rosai went to the St. Petersburg ballet school where one of his classmates was Fedor Lopukhov. In contrast to the latter, Georgy Rosai became a successful dancer famous for his unusually high leaps and virtuoso technique. He took part in Sergei Diaghilev's Russian seasons in Paris and brilliantly performed grotesque parts in Michel Fokine's choreographic débuts.

Georgy Rosai's life, however, was short. He died at the age of thirty in Petrograd (Leningrad) in the first severe winter after the revolution of 1917.

His sister Claudia, who was also in love with ballet, got married in the 'twenties. In 1927 she gave birth to a boy, who was christened Yuri (Georgy) after his late uncle. That was Yuri Grigorovich, the future choreographer.

In 1927 Lopukhov produced his *Ice Maiden*. Exactly thirty years later Yuri Grigorovich made his début as a choreographer on the Kirov stage thanks to Lopukhov's initiative and assistance. His first ballet *The Stone Flower* put the finishing touches to the style roughly outlined by Lopukhov in *The Ice Maiden* and opened a new chapter in the history of Soviet ballet. Now Grigorovich was on the way to unravelling the mystery of *The Nutcracker*.

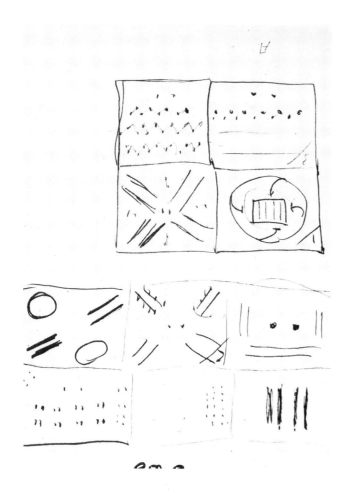

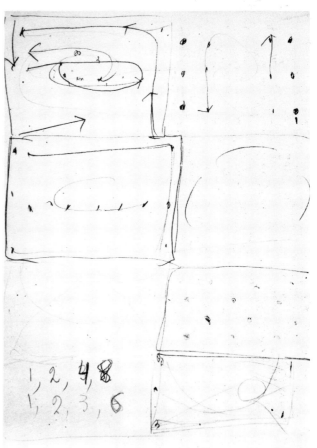

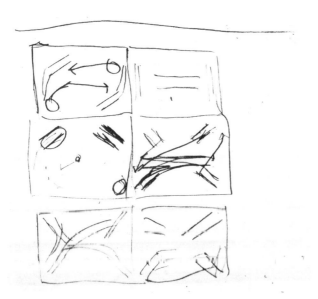

These drawings and notes are the originals which the author, Yuri Grigorovich made while working on his own version of *The Nutcracker*. This version is critically acclaimed as the best.

Moscow, 1966

The Nutcracker ushered in a new stage in Grigorovich's life and art. That was his first original production at the Bolshoi after he had been appointed its chief choreographer in 1964.

Here is the choreographer's own description of his conception of *The Nutcracker*.

"I knew, of course, that for a choreographer The Nutcracker *was a hard nut to crack. Its history seemed to be a chain of failures. Was it true that it was simply unfit for the stage, as it was claimed by some authorities on ballet? Some traced these setbacks to mistakes in the scenario, others to the choreographers' insensitiveness to the music or insufficient attention to the literary source.*

"At first I presumed that the scenario really needed a radical revision and that the music should also be re-examined from the viewpoint of the dramaturgy brought into line with the Hoffmann story.

"A careful study of the score, however, convinced me that Hoffmann and Tchaikovsky had in fact produced very different works, and the link between them was based on their inner affinity.

"What then would be the point of departure in my own version: the music, the tale, or my own ideas?

"The choice was easy to make. I had dreamt of staging The Nutcracker *of Tchaikovsky to express my own interpretation of his wonderful and mysterious music. I had to find an authentic equivalent for it in dance and theatrical action capable of revealing not my general ideas but my subjective perception of its world translated into the language of dance.*

"In other words, I wholly entrusted myself to Tchaikovsky's score. That was why I said in an interview after the première: 'I simply listened to the music and followed its guidelines'.

"In this light I viewed the scenario. A faithful sensation of the logic of musical development was to give me the clue to the dramaturgy of the ballet. The amazing integrity of the composer's conception secured the links of the score with the Hoffmann story. I remembered that supplementing the ballet with details of the plot in Lopukhov's and Vainonen's versions had not added to a more profound interpretation of the music. I decided, therefore, to search only for new emotional nuances of individual scenes to enhance the atmosphere of Hoffmann's tale.

"I realized that a choreographer determined to come up with his own version of The Nutcracker *is obliged to abandon any preconceived notions and heed the voice of his own instinct."*

Grigorovich, however, does not rely on intuition and improvization alone. He plans his productions with mathematical precision and prepares every rehearsal in minute detail, clearly defining the task, style and character of the episode or scene to be staged. This does not rule out improvization in the process of rehearsals, of course. A scene impeccably planned at home may reveal flaws demanding a revision. But he never loses sight of his purpose, which is one of his most striking features as a choreographer.

He has an amazing gift for dramaturgy and can see in his mind's eye all the details of the future production. Therefore, he is unexcelled in staging large-scale ballets which require a faultless organization of action.

He analyzes the music piecemeal, as it were, taking account of the orchestration and the significance of every instrument for a given episode and paying special attention to the "links" between scenes and the entrées of characters, which is crucial to the integrity of a production.

The composition of dances and the choreographic text are preceded by a long period of preparatory work. He studies all available material on the ballet---the history of former productions, if any, the epoch portrayed in it, the historical traditions and the roots of the literary source. The study of related material gives rise to new ideas and mantal associations that may be valuable to the future production. At this stage he listens to the music and analyzes it musicologically. He seems to feel that the music gradually sinks into his subconscious, stirring his emotions and forming a general artistic vision of stage events. Grigorovich describes this process in this phrase: *"I understand what is going on here but I'm yet unable to see it."* His perception of the music and his imagination blend into visual scenes in his mind.

The Prologue

The overture to the ballet is played with the curtains drawn. They are raised with the first bars of the theme of the assembly of guests. The empty proscenium is separated from the rest of the stage by a special stage curtain bearing a fantastic fir tree pattern. After a pause, guests make their appearance on the proscenium. This is a fragment of the action accurately harmonized with the rhythm of the music.

There is a sequence of genre and grotesque scenes, each with a distinctive pattern of movement. Staid and solemn adult guests are followed by young girls mincing on tiptoe and boys at a marching step. Two gossiping ladies, also on tiptoe, are exchanging news and are pulled apart by their daughters, but they try in vain. Three foppish young men are followed by a stiff respectable lady and a playful gentleman who has obviously had a couple of drinks before going to the Christmas party. The girls and ladies are dressed in capes and the boys have tricorns on their heads. The stage lights create the illusion of a snowfall. The scenery is gay and picturesque. Simon Virsaladze, who designs all of Grigorovich's ballets, has subtly depicted the atmosphere of a burgher's style of life with its luxury of details in the interior and cosy dwelling comfort.

Drosselmeier wearing a top hat, with a walking stick and the Nutcracker toy in his hands is the last guest to come. He is a grotesque character dressed in a black frock-coat with a lemon-colored vest and gloves to match. The Nutcracker is a bright red monster with very short legs and arms.

Drosselmeier raises the toy to show it to the audience and disappears. The proscenium curtain is raised, and we can see the sitting-room in Masha's home. The guests are already assembled here. Amid general confusion and merry-making the children run up to the front of the stage and a huge Christmas tree lights up in the background.

The children stand still for a moment, then quickly fall into line for their first marching dance together with the boys led by Masha's brother. The girls form a ring around Masha in the stage center, and the boys form ranks on the rest of the stage. The boys perform a "war dance" imitating goose-stepping soldiers and the girls look like dancers in a puppet show. *These are two different dances to the same music!*

Grigorovich deliberately simplified events by discarding masquerade costumes and masks of the children, the dinner table for the adult guests, and the intricate system of curtains to do away with superfluous genre details that would have made the scene too complicated.

Drosselmeier, Masha and the Nutcracker

Drosselmeier is a central figure in the ballet. In his draft notes Grigorovich describes his part and costume in the minutest detail. With this character are connected the culminations of the action---the night scenes of the fantastic growth of the Christmas tree, the battle between the toy soldiers and the mice, and the Nutcracker's transformation into a prince. Drosselmeier brings to life and directs the world of the ballet. The habitual real world mysteriously changes in response to his magic signs.

Masha's dream is her vision of fantastic life. She is an unusual little girl who can see what is invisible to others. She can live in a world of phantoms and inspire life into inanimate objects. The Christmas tale is a story of faith in miracles and a dream of transfiguration. Here Grigorovich has identified what makes the essence of Tchaikovsky's music.

The fantastic world of the ballet created by Drosselmeier is presented as the heroine's fantasy. The boys who attended the Christmas party and her playmates turn into toy soldiers, the dolls accompany her in her magic journey. In her imagination lifeless things come to life, the Christmas Tree and the room grow larger and larger, the sky expands into limitless vastness, and the stars dance a waltz. And finally, her rag toy transforms into a handsome fairy tale prince.

In her first entrée at the Christmas party Masha seems to be a doll herself. The space of her dance is limited, her steps are almost mechanical, and all her movements are small and careful. She is a home child but she longs for a different life of freedom.

In the night scene the world changes mysteriously under the spell of Drosselmeier's magic. The growing Christmas tree symbolizes her desire to get to know more about what is a mystery to her. Large jetés appear in her dance as she hovers over the vast space of the empty stage. She frees herself of her puppet-like image, her home and the long-familiar routine of daily life. Her dormant feelings are awakened and she is eager to become as free as a snowflake, as one of the myriads of stars in the endless sky, to escape from her earthly fate.

That motif was very close to Tchaikovsky. That was a motif of freedom from convention, a flight from reality, an escape from oneself in quest of a different and happy life.

The beautiful Prince, however, is an ephemeral dream, a phantom like a flimsy candlelight on the Christmas tree. It is a promise of love that is not fulfilled. He calls her to the distant stars but leaves her alone with her dream.

The Prince is happy with his triumph and thankful for her sacrifices but he is absolutely free of any commitments. real or imagined. In the scene of his release from the spell of witchcraft he seems to admire his newly-gained image. The dolls bow before him in reverence. And Masha herself stands still in delight before this perfect being she has created.

Unlike Hoffmann's Marie she is not destined to become the Queen of the Kingdom of Sweets. She knows that the Prince is a phantom who will vanish into thin air with the first rays of the morning sun. Her beautiful dream never comes true.

The Battle of the Toys and Mice

This is the most abstruse episode in the music. Grigorovich's drafts of the battle show that he imagined it as a scene of fierce fighting with naturalistic details: "a rat with a dead toy in its teeth", "a beheaded doll", "a rat with its tail cut off", etc. These ugly incidents were suggested by the music. In his production, however, he gave up this plan in favor of a symbolic battle between puppet-like fighters.

The groups of combatants are arranged symmetrically in keeping with the classical principle of ensemble dance. The fighters never come in contact with each other. The illusion of a battle is created by a conflict between different leitmotifs of dance. The toy soldiers' steps are steady and measured with mechanical regularity, the movements of mice are stealthy and treacherous. Both sides occasionally perform identical pas (emboîté, échappé) which imitate each other as though in a curved mirror. There are elements of acrobatics in the dances of mice, and toy soldiers perform intricate virtuoso pas, such as revoltade leaps, which are fairly difficult even for a soloist, but here they are executed by the whole corps de ballet.

The Waltz of Snowflakes

Grigorovich gave a new interpretation to the *Waltz of Snowflakes* by making Masha and the Prince its active participants. They have their own theme in the waltz which continues the story of their love.

The Spanish, Indian, Chinese, and other dolls saved in the battle are playing with snow and throwing it into the air. Little by little they leave the stage and Masha and the Prince remain alone. Their duet is pervaded with intonations of mutual gratitude and affection.

The whole corps de ballet of snowflakes appears on the stage. Dancers in tutus and snow-white hats topped with pompons surround the hero and heroine beginning their first love dialogue. Snowflakes take up and develop the motifs of their dance.

The *Waltz of Snowflakes* is based on a strictly geometric pattern. The hero and heroine describe a magic square in the empty space of the stage---a series of glissades along the small diagonals crowned with a large diagonal of supports in romantic style.

Their dance creates the image of a soaring flight. Its strictly geometric pattern means total harmony of body and soul and the achievement of an ideal. The waltz culminates in two circles of jete en tournant. Masha and the Prince fly towards each other past a snowdrift formed by dancing snowflakes. They meet in the finale, and the snowflakes gather around them as if to shelter them from the blizzard. They begin their journey up the Christmas tree in a magic boat escorted by snowflakes. It is a journey to the stars.

The Adagio

The waltz of the stars, which is the rosy waltz in Tchaikovsky's music, crowns the ballet and leads up to the adagio of Masha and the Nutcracker. Candles seem to be floating in dance, groups of female and male soloists solemnly follow each other as a prelude to the culmination.

Masha wearing a tutu appears from the right-hand wing and comes to the stage center to meet the Prince in front of the altar formed by the corps de ballet. They kneel before it as if in prayer. The adagio is choreographed as a wedding ritual.

The fairy tale comes to an end. Masha and the Prince raised to the stars stretch their arms towards one another as they dissolve in fading light. Their variations in the pas de deux are an elegiac dance of two loving hearts parting forever.

It is the end of a dream, a farewell to childhood. The tragic appeal of Tchaikovsky's music is expressed in dance with amazing veracity.

The Dancers

Grigorovich's production of *The Nutcracker* had its first night on March 12, 1966. Since then it has been an invariable item on the Bolshoi repertoire. One of his most popular and best known ballets, *The Nutcracker* has been staged by the Bolshoi company in the United States, Britain, France, Italy and other countries. At the Opera House of Vienna where it was produced under Grigorovich's direction, *The Nutcracker* was admired as much as in Moscow. It has had over one hundred performances at the Bolshoi.

First-class dancers appeared in the première with Ekaterina Maximova as Masha and Vladimir Vasilyev as the Prince. Maximova, one of the most charming ingénue dancers, subtly conveyed the genre nuances of Masha's image. She kept the audience spellbound by her childish spontaneity and sincerity. Vasilyev faithfully expressed the choreographer's idea of the character he danced: a combination of human and puppet elements, an incorporeal dream with chivalrous grace and manful elegance. His dance had triumphant intonations, freedom and impeccable virtuosity.

In the second cast these parts were danced by Nina Sorokina and Mikhail Lavrovsky. Sorokina, a neat and virtuoso dancer, suggested dramatic intonations in Masha's image. Lavrovsky created a heroic character of *The Nutcracker* as a brave warrior, a knight without fear and without reproach.

Later practically all leading dancers of the Bolshoi ballet joined the cast of *The Nutcracker*, Yuri Vladimirov and Vyacheslav Gordeyev as the Prince and Lyudmila Semenyaka and Nadezhda Pavlovas as Masha.

In 1968 Natalie Bessmertnova, the Bolshoi's most romantic ballerina with body lines of rare beauty, a keen sense of dance and music, made her début in the part of Masha. That was one of her finest achievements. The image conceived by Tchaikovsky and translated into the language of dance by Grigorovich was brought to perfection by Bessmertnova. She created a profoundly poetical character and revealed the romantic conflict between dreams and reality with crystal clarity. Her heroine is a nervous and anxious girl whose faith in miracles opens her eyes to the drama of life.

The part of Drosselmeier has been danced by many brilliant soloists, but Vladimir Levashev, who danced in the première and has now quit the stage, is remembered as superior to all.

Young dancers join the cast every year. Among the latest debutantes two are the most remarkable ones: Irina Arkhipova as Masha and Andris Liepa as the Nutcracker.

Grigorovich has given *The Nutcracker* a new lease of life, and growing numbers of ballet lovers come to appreciate the immortal beauty of this creation of Russian genius.

A Challenge to the Young

Grigorovich had this to say in an interview long after the première of *The Nutcracker* on March 12, 1966:

"At the time of producing The Nutcracker I was greatly fascinated by Hoffmann's tales and dreamt of other ballets on his motifs. In time my infatuation with his fantastic world and grotesquerie died down. It might have been a flame of youth.

"In my later work I took more interest in epic and historical themes. But The Nutcracker *is impressed on my memory as one of the happiest events in my life.*

"I don't know if I would like to come back to this ballet. I would rather not. I realize, of course, that it is largely a mystery to this day. But I believe that it is up to choreographers of the future to unriddle its blank spots.

"It is clear that The Nutcracker *cannot be staged as a routine production just because its music is so beautiful and its subject so fascinating and offering good chances for an imaginative mind.*

"It is my strong belief that an irresistible inner motive to embrace its hidden meaning is a must to whoever wants to handle this ballet. That should be an urge like the one Tchaikovsky felt in composing it. This may be the work of a lifetime."

It had taken *The Nutcracker* almost seventy-five years to establish itself on the Russian ballet stage. Grigorovich's production returned the ballet to its sources and ushered in the modern history of the Bolshoi ballet with its brilliant achievements under his innovative direction.

March 12, 1966 is indeed a red-letter day for the Russian ballet world.

It is the day before Christmas and the dream of dreams comes true . . . this will be a white Christmas! The snowflakes are falling . . . gently, quietly . . . everything is gradually covered with beautiful white snow.

Yuri Grigorovich, the principal choreographer and artistic director of the Bolshoi Theatre. Photo by Michel Szabo.

57

The magic of Christmas begins as the snowflakes become Snow Maidens ... these beautiful white Snow Fairies dance about the stage like snowflakes dancing in the wind.

Christmastime is celebrated with a
beautiful Christmas tree, whitened by
snowflakes, with lovely gifts and
magnificent decorations.

At Marie's home, the Stahlbaums have erected their Christmas tree, too. It is not white, however, because it is indoors, but it is magnificently decorated with lots of toys and presents for Marie and her brother, Fritz. As on a typical Christmas eve, everything is in place awaiting the arrival of the special friends who will bring gifts for the Stahlbaum children.

For some reason the Christmas tree has a military look about it. Under the tree is a toy soldier's riding horse, a military bugle and drum, and a mysterious clock built by the toymaker and magician Uncle Drosselmeier. Soon Uncle Drosselmeier will come with the most fascinating toys.

All the friends have arrived and the children have received their Christmas gifts . . . they are so happy that they start dancing, the boys flashing their toy swords and the girls playing with their new dolls.

Marie is the happiest of all . . . she has a new white dress . . . and she proudly dances in front of her friends showing it off.

The parents of the children send the children off to play hide-and-seek . . . then the parents start dancing, displaying their own holiday finery.

Suddenly, a chilling silence announces the arrival
of the most mysterious guest of all. In spite of his
mask, everyone recognizes Uncle Drosselmeier.
He is a genius who makes talking clocks and
mechanical toys . . . he also performs all kinds of
magic. What kind of magic will be presented for
everybody's entertainment tonight? No one
knows yet . . . perhaps even Uncle Drosselmeier
doesn't quite know what will happen.

Uncle Drosselmeier takes center stage as all the children crowd around for a better view of his stunts and tricks. First he balances himself in a sitting position on one foot and his magic cane.

Then, mystery of mysteries, he walks away from his cane and still it stands up unsupported! Even the parents cannot figure out how he does these wonderful things. But this is just the beginning . . .

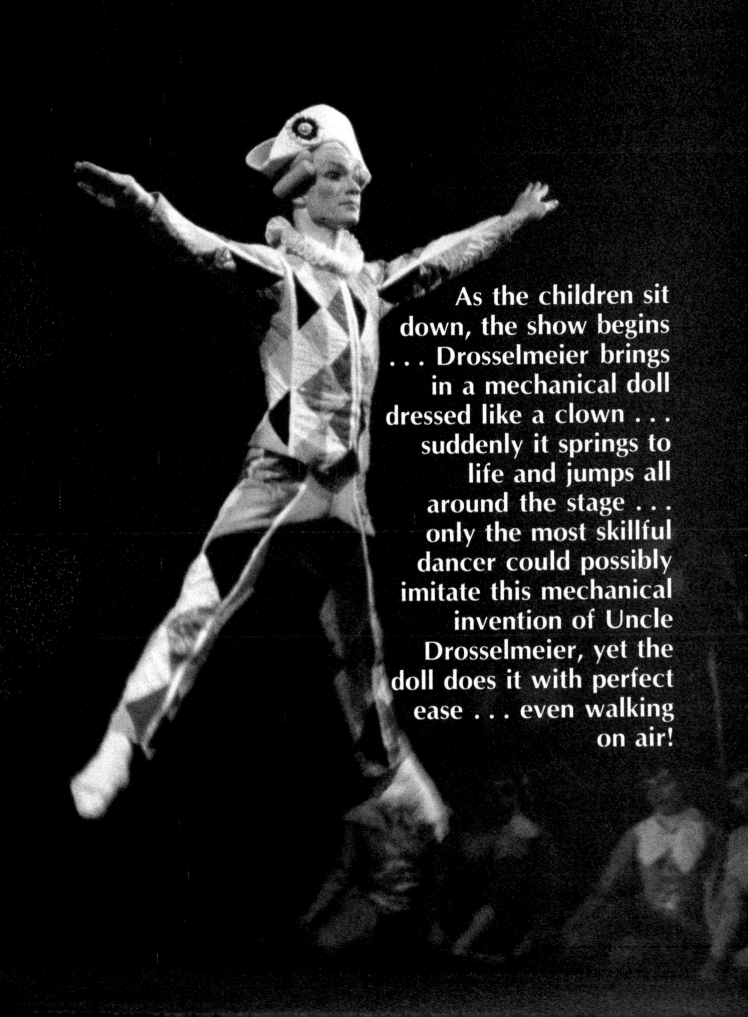

As the children sit down, the show begins . . . Drosselmeier brings in a mechanical doll dressed like a clown . . . suddenly it springs to life and jumps all around the stage . . . only the most skillful dancer could possibly imitate this mechanical invention of Uncle Drosselmeier, yet the doll does it with perfect ease . . . even walking on air!

As the clown bounces out of view and vanishes into thin air, two more mechanical dolls come to life. These are little elves who dance together and around each other in a most mischievous way ... all the children laugh at the comical dances and expressions on the elves' faces. What a wondrous time everyone is having ... but how does Uncle Drosselmeier do it? Will there be more magic?

Suddenly Uncle Drosselmeier brings in a huge doll, dressed in a beautiful red military uniform. This, Uncle Drosselmeier explains, is his special Christmas present for Marie. Unfortunately, the doll's face is not handsome for his nose is large and his mouth is huge. Uncle Drosselmeier explains that he has a special mouth . . . so strong it can crack nuts . . . therefore, he says, this is a toy mechanical nutcracker. Marie loves the doll at once, but her brother Fritz is terribly jealous because he didn't get a present . . . so he attacks the Nutcracker and gleefully breaks it.

Marie is broken-hearted and starts to cry. But Uncle Drosselmeier immediately comes to the rescue. He lifts the
broken Nutcracker from the floor and, helped by Marie,
examines him carefully. "Yes, the Nutcracker can be
fixed," says Uncle Drosselmeier, "so you children must
all go to sleep now and when you awake in the morning,
the Nutcracker will be mended and in perfect condition."
Marie helps Uncle Drosselmeier carry the broken Nutcracker away.

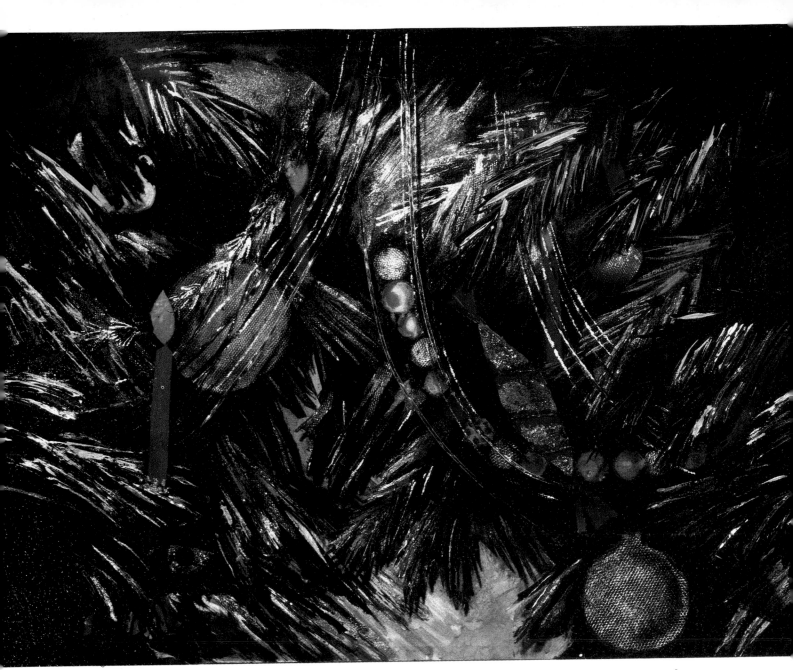

It is surprising to Marie that Uncle Drosselmeier selects
the Christmas tree under which to place the broken Nutcracker doll. But Uncle Drosselmeier explains that this is
the safest place for him because this is not an ordinary
Christmas tree, but a magical tree. Marie isn't quite convinced of this; she is afraid that her brother Fritz will return and do more damage to her beloved Nutcracker. So
she stays with the Nutcracker under the Christmas Tree
and soon falls sound asleep, extremely tired from her
emotional experiences.

Then the miracles begin
to happen . . . the green
tree slowly grows . . .
and grows . . . until it
fills the whole room . . .
it turns white, too . . .
and all the toys grow,
too. The rocking
horse becomes as
large as a
normal horse
. . . and the
dolls become
as big as
real people.

Then, all alone, Uncle Drosselmeier appears. Of course this is all in Marie's dream world, but she believes it is really happening. Suddenly there is a large flash of light and a miniature explosion . . . a huge flame and column of smoke suddenly appear out of nowhere. This is surely another magic trick of Uncle Drosselmeier's.

From this smoke suddenly there appears a huge black monster Mouse King. So frightening is his appearance that all the terrified toys run away. Only Uncle Drosselmeier stays, posing as a servant awaiting the wishes of the Mouse King.

The Mouse King summons his army of ugly mouse soldiers . . . and soon the entire stage is filled with them.

Marie is terrified ... but Uncle Drosselmeier's magic goes to work and the Nutcracker comes to life. He springs to his feet, jumps on the horse, blows the bugle and all the toy soldiers return, take out their swords and join the Nutcracker in his fight against the Mouse King and his army.

As the fighting goes on, the Mouse King and the Nutcracker finally meet in a duel to the death.

Marie sees this horrible fight from the sidelines . . . everything is getting out of control! Even Uncle Drosselmeier is unable to stop the slaughter as the Mouse King's army overwhelms the toy soldiers. Marie cannot allow the Mouse King to kill her beloved Nutcracker!! In desperation, she picks up a heavy, lighted candlestick and with all her strength throws it at the Mouse King. This so frightens the Mouse King that he runs away, with his mouse army following him.

The toy soldiers are victorious!!! How happy they are!! They glorify Marie and carry her on their shoulders. Little does she know that her manifestation of love for the ugly Nutcracker breaks a magic curse put on him by the Mouse Queen many years before ... suddenly the Nutcracker's face begins to change from an ugly, odd doll into a handsome real-life Prince.

Everybody is joyously happy . . . they surround the Prince and Marie . . . and the Snowflake Fairies return with their beautiful dance . . .

As a gift and tribute to Marie for saving their lives, all the toys want to do something to show their gratitude, so each group of dolls presents her with a special dance. First, the Spanish dolls perform a fiery Spanish dance . . .

And the exotic Indian dolls, in their elaborate costumes, suddenly perform a very unfamiliar acrobatic dance which only the most skilled dancers can accomplish.

But one of the most spectacular dances is that of the Chinese dolls. These are the favorite dolls of the world and everybody recognizes them immediately. How high they jump!

And how lovely are the shepherd and shepherdess, with their sheep. Their dance is so lovely . . . slow . . . and peaceful. It is called a *"pastorale."* The dancers have great skill for they must do as much acting as dancing. Everybody watches their beautiful dancing very closely.

More and more dolls and toys crowd the stage as a pair of Russian dolls, dressed in Russian folk costumes of old, dance traditional steps.

As a grand finale, all the dancing dolls get together, celebrating their new friend Marie and the very handsome Prince. Life, at the moment, seems to be a bowl of cherries!

Suddenly Marie's attention is drawn to the toy boat hanging from the Christmas tree. As she stares in disbelief, it grows larger and larger, so large in fact that it is now a full-sized ship. The Prince takes Marie's hand and they slowly board the ship, waving good-bye to the dolls and telling them they are off to the Kingdom of Sweets.

Beautiful fairies welcome Marie and the Prince to the Kingdom of Sweets. This is a land of kindness and honesty . . . there is no place for evil here!

Soon handsome Pages appear and dance their welcome to the Prince and Marie. "Welcome to the Kingdom of Sweets" . . . the Land where there is no evil . . .

"We hear no evil . . . see no evil . . . and do no evil. Wel-come, welcome, you are safe here from the Mouse King."

The Fairies and the Pages dance together as they are told to prepare for a royal wedding, for the Prince has proposed to Marie and they shortly will be married in a royal wedding ceremony full of pomp, music and dancing.

Soon the handsome Prince and Marie are ready for the wedding ceremony. The Pages surround them with their magic candles. Everything is so beautiful and wonderful . . .

... that the couple begins to dance in joy ...

. . . everybody is so happy
for this royal marriage.

The Prince tells his story. He speaks of the great love which was necessary to transform him from an ugly doll into a handsome young man.

He tells of the curse of the Mouse Queen . . . and he tells
how love can conquer all obstacles.

Marie is also very happy. She dances joyously and wants everyone to share her happiness with her.

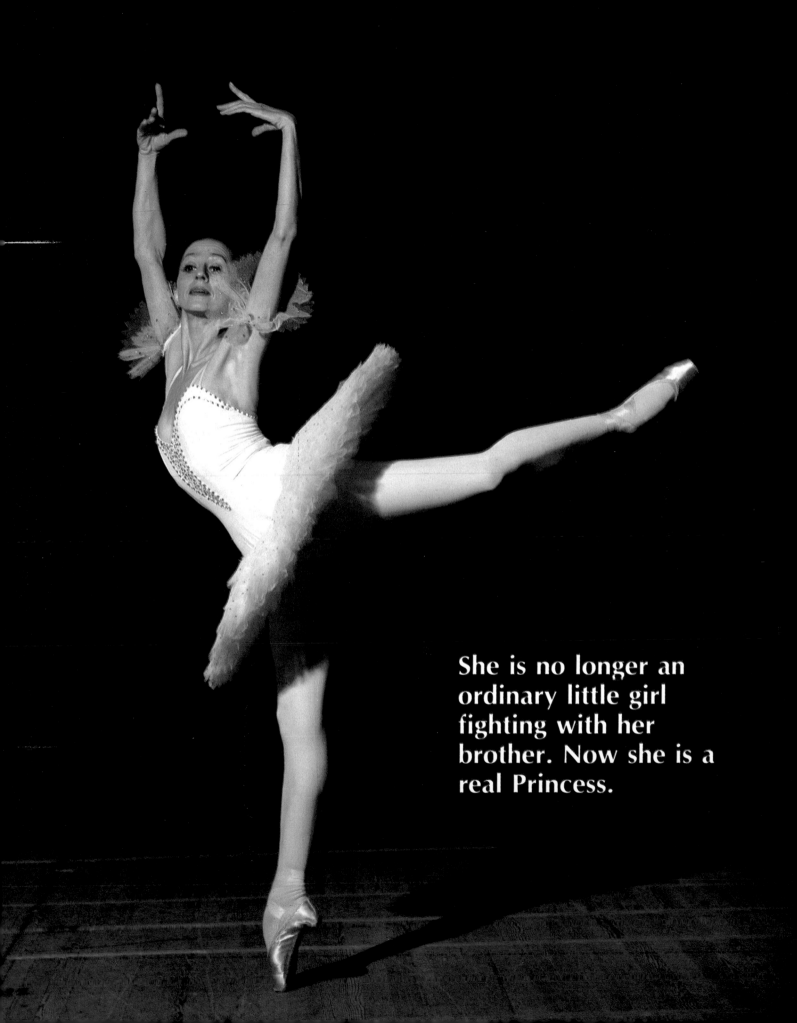

She is no longer an ordinary little girl fighting with her brother. Now she is a real Princess.

She won this great honor because she loved and cared for the Nutcracker.

She never did care
whether the
Nutcracker was
handsome or not.

She loved him for his warm heart and gentleness . . . the qualities that last forever, since everyone knows that being young, handsome or beautiful is only a fleeting thing.

The Prince agrees with her and promises to return her love for as long as they both shall live ... the same promise that lovers still make to each other.

For whatever befalls one, the other will always be there to help. Life can be complete only when it is shared in partnership.

The Prince will be honest and faithful and always extend his hand in love and respect . . . his support for his beautiful Princess will be strong and everlasting. She need never fear any evil forces, especially the Mouse King!

As the marriage ceremony continues, they swear vow after vow ... love, honor, cherish ... all the wonderful principles upon which marriages are based. The Pages lift the royal couple in the air so all may hear the marriage vows.

In the grand ending of
the ceremony, the
Prince demonstrates his
strength. He will always
be there when his new
Princess wife needs him.

The Fairies throw the wedding veil over Marie's head and the brightness from the huge candles light the way back to reality as she and the Prince walk into the darkness.

Alas! Every dream comes to an end. Marie shudders and wakes up. Her Nutcracker doll is still in her arms . . . still broken . . . but she knows that by closing her eyes when she sleeps in her warm bed, she can always bring her handsome Prince back to her . . . and together they can visit the Kingdom of Sweets to fulfill their marriage vows . . . love . . . honor . . . and cherish.